W9-BMB-843

AR level 4.2
pts 1/2

CHIHUAHUAS

By Tammy Gagne

Consultant: Carolyn Mooney
Emeritus Judge
American Kennel Club

Capstone
press

Mankato, Minnesota

Edge Books are published by Capstone Press,
151 Good Counsel Drive, P.O. Box 669, Mankato, Minnesota 56002.
www.capstonepress.com

Library of Congress Cataloging-in-Publication Data
Gagne, Tammy.
    Chihuahuas / by Tammy Gagne.
    p. cm. — (Edge books. All about dogs)
    Includes bibliographical references and index.
    ISBN-13: 978-1-4296-1947-9 (hardcover)
    ISBN-10: 1-4296-1947-3 (hardcover)
    1. Chihuahua (Dog breed) — Juvenile literature. I. Title. II. Series.
SF429.C45G28 2009
636.76 — dc22   2008001222

Summary: Describes the history, physical features, temperament, and care of
    the Chihuahua breed.

Editorial Credits
Erika L. Shores, editor; Veronica Bianchini, designer; Marcie Spence,
    photo researcher

Photo Credits
AP Images/Las Cruces Sun-News, Norm Dettlaff, 18
Capstone Press/Karon Dubke, cover, 1, 7, 16, 25, 26, 27
Dreamstime/Jszg005, 15 (right); Pixbuilder, 17
Getty Images Inc./GK Hart/Vikki Hart, 29
iStockphoto/Gary Caviness, 20; Rich Legg, 12
Nature Picture Library/Petra Wegner, 24
Peter Arnold/Gerard Lacz, 19; William Campbell, 9
Ron Kimball Stock/Richard Stacks, 6
Shutterstock/Annette, 23; Gertjan Hooijer, 21; Hagit Berkovich, 11; Matt Apps, 5;
    Pavitra, 14; pixshots, 15 (left); WizData, Inc., 13

**Capstone Press thanks Martha Diedrich, dog trainer, for her assistance
    with this book.**

1 2 3 4 5 6 13 12 11 10 09 08

Printed in the United States of America in Stevens Point, Wisconsin.

072009
005595R

Table of Contents

CHAPTER 1

A TINY DOG

For the smallest dog breed in the world, the Chihuahua has a long name. But don't let its small size fool you. This little dog has a big personality. Chihuahuas are extremely popular pets. The tiny dogs are friendly, intelligent, and loads of fun

Chihuahuas may be little, but they do most of the things bigger dogs do. They go for walks, chase balls, and chew bones. But this breed isn't right for everyone. The first step toward becoming a Chihuahua owner is learning as much as you can about this unique breed.

The Chihuahua is a member of the toy group. The word "toy" means the breed is small. It doesn't mean the dog can be handled like a toy. Toy breeds should be handled gently. Yelling or running toward a small dog may frighten it.

The little Chihuahua is a popular pet throughout the United States.

Chihuahua puppies weigh less than an apple at birth.

Finding a Chihuahua

The best way to find a Chihuahua puppy is through a breeder. A local Chihuahua breed club can give you a list of good breeders in your area. A breed club helps teach its members and the public about a dog breed.

Adoption is another way to find a Chihuahua. Animal shelters and breed rescue groups help match people looking for Chihuahuas with dogs that need new homes.

When searching for a Chihuahua, look for a healthy and friendly pup. Healthy Chihuahuas have shiny coats, bright eyes, and wagging tails. They do not cough or have runny noses.

breeder — someone who breeds and raises dogs or other animals

CHAPTER 2

CHIHUAHUA HISTORY

Many beliefs exist about the origins of the Chihuahua. No one knows for sure which idea is correct. People do agree that the breed was named after the Mexican state of Chihuahua. Most people believe Chihuahuas came from this area. Others think the breed's roots lie farther away.

All dogs today share a single ancestor — the wolf. Some scientists have traced the Chihuahua back to the Mexican gray wolf. This small wolf has lived in North America for thousands of years. If this ancestry is correct, the Chihuahua could be the oldest dog breed on the continent.

Chihuahuas could be related to the Mexican gray wolf.

The Chihuahua looks more like a tiny fox than a wolf. It resembles an African animal called the fennec fox. This desert creature has huge ears and large eyes. It weighs only 3 pounds (1.4 kilograms). Could the Chihuahua be related to the fennec fox? Some people think so. Bones of a dog similar to the Chihuahua were once found in a 3,000-year-old tomb in Egypt.

Other people believe the first Chihuahuas came from Europe. A tiny dog breed once lived on the island of Malta. This dog had a soft spot on its head like some modern Chihuahuas do. This spot is called a molera. Moleras are rare in other dog breeds.

Still others think Chihuahuas could have arrived in Mexico from China. Chinese trade ships made many trips to Mexico in the 1700s and 1800s. This idea is unlikely, though, since Chihuahuas lived in Mexico long before this time period.

The Chihuahua's Mexican History

The Toltec tribe ruled northern and central Mexico from 900 to 1150. The Toltecs owned small dogs they called Techichi. These dogs were only slightly larger than today's Chihuahua. Pyramid carvings of the Techichi look very much like the Chihuahua.

Techichi were valued as companions. Some owners even believed their dogs could join them in the afterlife. Bones of Techichi have been found alongside human skeletons in Mexican graves. People often wanted to be buried with their dogs after they died. Sadly, this sometimes meant that dogs were killed when their owners died. Other times, only statues of the dogs were placed in the graves.

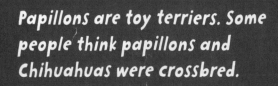

Papillons are toy terriers. Some people think papillons and Chihuahuas were crossbred.

The first Chihuahuas were brought into the United States in the late 1800s. They were called Texas dogs or Arizona dogs after the states where the Mexican dogs crossed the U.S. border.

One belief was that these dogs were bred with other small dogs to develop the Chihuahua breed. Today's Chihuahuas may have been crossbred with papillons and pomeranians.

The first Chihuahua was registered with the American Kennel Club (AKC) in 1904. The breed is now one of the most popular dogs in the country. More than 22,000 Chihuahuas were registered with the AKC in 2006.

A pomeranian's face is similar to a Chihuahua's face.

crossbreed — to mate two different breeds of dogs

13

CHAPTER 3

FRIENDLY AND FUN-LOVING DOGS

A Chihuahua is easy to recognize because of its big, pointed ears.

People have many reasons to love Chihuahuas. These lively little dogs are cute, playful, and brave. The breed's body may be little, but its outgoing personality is anything but small.

Physical Features

Chihuahuas have friendly faces. Their big eyes are a huge part of their kind look. The dog's ears are large and pointed.

An adult Chihuahua typically weighs less than 6 pounds (3 kilograms). Most Chihuahuas measure between 6 and 9 inches (15 and 23 centimeters) tall. Even a newborn baby is larger than most Chihuahuas. But Chihuahuas have muscular bodies and are surprisingly strong for their size.

Chihuahuas come in a variety of colors. These include black, chocolate, cream, white, and fawn. A fawn coat is tan. A Chihuahua may also be **brindle** or a combination of colors, such as black and tan.

Chihuahuas with short hair are called smooth-coated dogs. Smooth-coated Chihuahuas and long-coated Chihuahuas are often born in the same litters.

brindle — a fawn coat with black stripes

Temperament

The combination of a dog's personality and behavior is called its temperament. A friendly dog is said to have a good nature or temperament. In general, Chihuahuas are outgoing, intelligent, and highly trainable. But every dog is different. Dogs that have been mistreated may have more aggressive temperaments. These dogs do not make good family pets.

Chihuahuas form strong bonds with their owners. They may even begin to dislike others who are close to their favorite people. This makes training very important. A dog should always understand that it's not the boss. Teaching a dog to follow commands lets the dog know its owner is in charge.

Most Chihuahuas have friendly, good-natured temperaments.

Chihuahuas love learning new tricks and exploring new places. Certainly, one of the bonuses of owning a Chihuahua is the breed's portable size. Yet many Chihuahuas enjoy walking on a leash much more than being carried. Be careful when walking your dog around other animals. Even a friendly larger dog could accidentally hurt a Chihuahua.

Even little dogs like Chihuahuas enjoy walking on a leash.

Chihuahuas need only a small amount of exercise daily. On rainy days, a short play period indoors is enough. When the weather is better, outdoor play is best. Fresh air is good for a dog's health. A fenced yard can make exercise easier, but a Chihuahua is too little to ever be left outside alone. A Chihuahua is small enough to escape through the tiniest gap in a fence.

Small toys keep
a Chihuahua busy
when it's alone.

EDGE FACT

A Chihuahua sometimes gets
the shivers when it's cold,
excited, or scared.

Most Chihuahuas don't enjoy being left alone indoors for long periods of time. Some owners choose to send their dogs to a doggie day care. A doggie day care is a great way for a Chihuahua to get the attention and exercise it needs during the day. Otherwise, owners should provide their Chihuahuas with plenty of toys to keep them busy while they're home alone.

Having another dog or cat in the household to play with can be fun for any pet. Chihuahuas usually get along well with most other pets when they have been raised together. Larger dogs or even cats with poor temperaments can be dangerous, however. The best choice for a friend for a Chihuahua is another Chihuahua.

Playful Chihuahuas get along best with other Chihuahuas.

CHAPTER 4

CARING FOR A CHIHUAHUA

Owning a dog can be great fun. It is also a lot of hard work. Chihuahuas have many needs. It's up to the dog's owner to meet these needs.

Make a Shopping List

Several items top the Chihuahua's list of supplies. The first is a collar and leash. Both should be lightweight and fit well. Next, every dog needs a set of food and water dishes.

A Chihuahua also needs its own bed. Some owners allow their dogs to sleep with them in their beds. This can be dangerous for a Chihuahua. Falling or jumping off a tall piece of furniture could hurt this small dog.

Toys make life fun and help pets pass the time when owners are away from home. Small, lightweight balls and squeak toys often are favorite toys for dogs. Remember your dog's size when choosing playthings. Toys shouldn't be so small that the dog swallows them.

An owner should provide a Chihuahua with its own bed.

Chihuahuas learn best
when they are rewarded
with treats or praise.

Training a Chihuahua

Some people think that small dogs do not need training. They couldn't be more wrong. All dogs need to learn to behave properly.

The best training methods are positive ones. Owners should praise their animals for doing what is expected. A Chihuahua should never be physically punished for making a mistake. That only teaches the dog to fear people.

Training can be done at home or with other owners and their dogs at an **obedience** class. In addition to "sit" and "stay," a well-trained Chihuahua should know the commands "down," "come," and "drop it."

EDGE FACT

A dog sweater can help keep a Chihuahua warm in cold weather.

obedience — obeying rules and commands

Feeding a Chihuahua

Chihuahuas need to be fed twice a day. If a Chihuahua eats too much, it can become overweight. Carrying extra weight can cause hip and knee problems. It can also lead to many diseases, such as diabetes and heart problems.

Dogs need to drink plenty of water. Owners should make sure fresh water is available to Chihuahuas all the time.

Grooming a Chihuahua

Long-coated Chihuahuas should be brushed every day to remove dirt and dead hair from their coats. Dogs with smooth coats need to be brushed once or twice a week. Soft-bristled brushes work best on both coat types.

Other grooming tasks are important. Chihuahuas need baths about once a month. Ears and eyes should be cleaned weekly to prevent infections. A Chihuahua's toenails should be trimmed every few weeks.

Trimming a Chihuahua's nails is an important grooming task.

Keeping a Chihuahua Healthy

A veterinarian is a person trained to treat sick or injured animals. A vet also helps healthy animals stay well. Taking a Chihuahua to a vet for a yearly exam is the best way to keep it healthy. Vets give dogs yearly vaccinations to prevent dangerous diseases. Vets also check for diseases common in the breed.

Another important step is having your Chihuahua spayed or neutered. This simple operation prevents the dog from ever having puppies. This helps control the pet population. It also lowers the animal's risk for many health problems, including cancer.

Properly caring for your dog will keep it healthy. Smaller dogs usually live longer than larger breeds. Many Chihuahuas have lived well into their late teens. A kind, caring owner can help a Chihuahua live a long, happy life.

EDGE FACT

Even dogs need clean teeth. Owners should brush their Chihuahua's teeth with a toothpaste made just for dogs.

A Chihuahua needs a yearly vet visit to stay healthy.

Glossary

breed (BREED) — a certain kind of animal within an animal group; breed also means to mate and raise a certain kind of animal.

breeder (BREE-duhr) — someone who breeds and raises dogs or other animals

brindle (BRIN-duhl) — a fawn coat with black stripes

crossbreed (KROSS-breed) — to mate two different dog breeds

obedience (oh-BEE-dee-uhnss) — obeying rules and commands

temperament (TEM-pur-uh-muhnt) — the combination of an animal's behavior and personality; the way an animal usually acts or responds to situations shows its temperament.

vaccination (vak-suh-NAY-shun) — a shot of medicine that protects animals from a disease

Read More

Gray, Susan H. *Chihuahuas*. Domestic Dogs. Chanhassen, Minn.: Child's World, 2007.

Miller, Richard, and Diane Morgan. *Chihuahuas*. The Animal Planet Pet Care Library. Neptune, N.J.: T.F.H. Publications, 2006.

Internet Sites

FactHound offers a safe, fun way to find Internet sites related to this book. All of the sites on FactHound have been researched by our staff.

Here's how:

1. Visit *www.facthound.com*
2. Choose your grade level.
3. Type in this book ID **1429619473** for age-appropriate sites. You may also browse subjects by clicking on letters, or by clicking on pictures and words.
4. Click on the **Fetch It** button.

FactHound will fetch the best sites for you!

Index